# WOMEN OF THE WEST

Volume 5

Tales of the Wild West Series

Rick Steber

Illustrations by Don Gray

NOTE
*WOMEN OF THE WEST* is the fifth book in the
Tales of the Wild West Series


*WOMEN OF THE WEST*
Volume 5
Tales of the Wild West Series

**Bonanza Publishing**
Box 204
Prineville, Oregon 97754

# Tales of the Wild West

# INTRODUCTION

Early-day women of the West are depicted in fading photographs: a gaunt, bonneted figure in a long dress walking beside a wagon, baby cradled in her arms, children scattered behind. She might be a woman stirring lye soap over an open fire, or a dance hall girl, or a homesteader's wife standing stoically beside her husband with the sod house in the background.

Letters and diaries tell the details of these women's lives; the sorrow of being uprooted from family and friends, the yearning for companionship of other women, bearing children without the benefit of a doctor and trying to rear them in an uncivilized land.

One turn-of-the-century western historian noted: "With the coming of woman came also the graces of life, better social order and conditions, and increased regard for the amenities of life."

Eastern women were relegated to conduct themselves within strictly-established social boundaries. Western women were allowed more freedom to stretch their wings and explore the realm of their existence. And in the process they were the ones who were responsible for taming the Wild West.

# SACAJAWEA

Sacajawea was born into the Shoshone tribe on the west side of the Rocky Mountains. When she was ten years old she was captured and enslaved by the Mandan tribe. At age fifteen she was purchased by Charboneau, a trapper with the North West Fur Company. In 1805 the Lewis and Clark Expedition employed Charboneau as an interpreter. Sacajawea accompanied her husband and carried her infant son, Jean Baptiste, on a cradleboard. She proved to be an inspiration to the men as they labored over the rugged terrain. Once, the canoe in which Sacajawea was riding was caught in rapids, tipped over and filled with water. The Indian girl had presence of mind to save herself and her baby, as well as grabbing a number of valuable items including scientific instruments, medicines and even the journals of the Expedition.

While crossing the Rocky Mountains and entering the land of the Shoshone, Sacajawea met with members of the tribe she had been stolen from. This meeting was a dramatic and emotional scene. She recognized a girl who had been captured with her so many years before, but had escaped; and, while acting as an interpreter, Sacajawea suddenly realized the chief was her own brother Cameahwait.

Sacajawea, often acting as interpreter and leading the way when others became disoriented, helped to bring the Expedition to the Pacific Ocean. She stayed through the winter and the following spring returned with the Expedition to the east side of the Rocky Mountains.

One account states Sacajawea died in 1812 but another claims she lived to be an old woman, dying in 1884 at the Wind River Indian Agency in Wyoming.

# MADAME DORION

Madame Marie Dorion was a full-blooded Sioux and the wife of Pierre Dorion, the half-breed interpreter for John Jacob Astor's overland expedition.

The Astor expedition got underway the spring of 1811 and Madame Dorion, with her two children, accompanied the men up the Missouri to the Black Hills, across the Rocky Mountains and down the Snake River until it swung north. It was on the last day of 1811, in the sagebrush hills near the present town of North Powder, Oregon, that the Dorion family dropped out of the rag-tag procession. Madame Dorion was in labor and at sunset she gave birth.

The following day the family rejoined the others who were camped in the Grande Ronde Valley feasting on dog meat purchased from the Indians. The party continued and after breaking trail through waist-deep snow in the Blue Mountains and unimaginable suffering, they reached the Umatilla River. Here the baby Dorion died and was buried.

Eventually the expedition reached Fort Astoria. In later years Pierre became a trapper and Madame Dorion and her children never left his side. They were with him in January 1814, trapping on the Malheur River, when Indians attacked and killed Pierre.

Madame Dorion escaped with her children and two horses. She set camp in a secluded ravine in the Blue Mountains, killed the horses and used the hides to build a shelter and for 53 days they subsisted solely on horsemeat. It was not until March that she was able to tramp over the mountains and reach a friendly village of Walla Walla Indians.

# MEDICINE WOMAN

The old woman, a Flathead Indian, was named Mary Sdipp-shin-mah, meaning "Fallen from the Sky". She was a medicine woman. "The spirit power came to me at a very young age," she explained through an interpreter. "I was five or six years old. Mother took me far up the mountain to pick huckleberries. Late in the afternoon she left me with instructions to stay and pick while she went farther.

"The sun set, but Mother did not return. It got dark. I was frightened, cried and slept on and off through the night. When the sun came up I thought I heard voices. I stopped crying and listened. From the timber I saw a woman and two children coming toward me. The woman said, 'Well, little girl, what are you doing? You must be lost.'

"She wore buckskins painted red and had trinkets around her neck. She led the way to the bottom of the gulch where I stopped to drink. I was very thirsty. Afterward I sat on the bank with the two children and the mother. She told me, 'Now I am going to take you back to your people. When you grow up you will be a medicine woman. I give you the power to heal people. I am your mother. This is your little brother and little sister.'

"I glanced away and when I looked back the mother and children were gone and in their place was a grizzly bear with two cubs sitting beside me. The bear said, 'I will take you to your people. Climb on my back.'

"I did. The bear ran very fast. After a while she stopped, told me, 'Your people are near. Walk a short distance and you will find them.' And I did.

"Now you know how I received the spirit power. My magic, my talisman comes from a bear's claw and a bit of fur I wear around my neck. I am medicine woman."

# FIRST WHITE WOMAN

Miss Jane Barnes was working as a barmaid in a drinking establishment in Portsmouth, England. One evening a customer, Donald McTavish, who had recently been appointed governor for the North West Fur Company in Oregon, suggested she accompany him to the far side of the world.

Historians have described Miss Barnes as having "flaxen hair and bright blue eyes" and they have written about her "curvaceous charms". It is without a doubt that after the *Isaac Todd* crossed the Columbia Bar on April 22, 1814 and dropped anchor at Fort George (Astoria), Miss Barnes, stepping from the rowboat to shore wearing a flowing dress, made a strong impression on the trappers and Indians.

Miss Barnes fielded several proposals of marriage. One of her admirers was Cassakas, son of Chinook chief Concomly. He promised to send 100 sea otter furs to her family, swore he would never ask her to draw water or dig roots and assured her she would be held in a revered position above his other four wives. She turned him down.

Miss Barnes also succeeded in making herself the subject of a jealous quarrel between Governor McTavish and young Alexander Henry, a fur trader with the North West Company. Both men, along with five sailors, were drowned attempting to cross the Columbia River during a storm.

After this tragedy Miss Barnes was returned to England where she was the center of attention, telling stories to the bar crowd about uncivilized Oregon. Miss Jane Barnes was the first white woman to set foot in the Pacific Northwest.

# INDIAN BRIDE

A young man came to the Oregon Country in the employ of the North West Fur Company and was assigned the position of clerk at a remote trading post. Within a few weeks he had met and proposed marriage to an Indian girl.

It was the native custom to purchase the bride from the bride's father, but in this case the father was deceased. The clerk bartered with the girl's mother. The woman demanded blankets, kettles and an array of trinkets.

The price was paid and preparations for the wedding began. The bride was bathed and, rather than wearing the fringed buckskin of her people, she dressed in a calico dress. As she made her way to the ceremonial fire, the clerk smiled broadly and congratulated himself on his wise choice for a mate.

At that inopportune moment an Indian who had been away hunting returned to camp. When the prospective bride saw him she ran away. The Indian rode directly to the clerk and without bothering to dismount he demanded to know, "Why try steal my wife?"

"No one told me she was married," protested the clerk. He offered to pay for his bride again, but the scorned husband refused, saying the faithlessness of his wife angered him and swore revenge against her.

At last a compromise was reached. For a rifle, one hundred rounds of ammunition, two kettles, three blankets, a dagger and several pounds of smoking tobacco the husband renounced all claim to his wife, freeing the clerk to marry his Indian bride.

# NARCISSA

Narcissa Prentiss was born in 1808 to strict Presbyterian parents. She converted to the church at age 10 and at 16 she read a book about missionary work and vowed to dedicate her life to her faith.

In 1831 a group of Indians, two Flathead and two Nez Perce, appeared in the East to ask for the "White Man's Book of Heaven". Their plea motivated Narcissa to volunteer to the American Board of Commissioners for Foreign Missions; she asked permission to carry Christianity to the Indians of the far West. The commissioners refused to send any "unmarried females".

It was mentioned, however, that Narcissa and Doctor Marcus Whitman, who had already been chosen to establish a mission among the Indians, would make suitable companions. They met and were attracted to each other. Shortly after their wedding they started west.

The Whitmans established their mission at Waiilatpu in the Walla Walla Valley. A log cabin was erected and four months later, in March 1837, Narcissa gave birth to Alice. The Indians called the baby "Little White Cayuse".

For two years Alice was a joy to her parents. And then one day she wandered away, fell into the nearby stream, and drowned. The loss of her only child opened Narcissa's heart to all children. In the fall of 1844 seven orphans — their parents had died crossing the Plains — were brought to Narcissa and she took them in.

In 1847 wagon train emigrants brought measles with them. Indians, who had no natural immunities to the disease, died by the thousands. Some Indians believed the white men were poisoning them and they attacked the mission. Fourteen people were killed, including Narcissa and Doctor Marcus Whitman.

# PIONEER SPEECH

Mrs. Robert Miller addressed the Oregon Pioneer Association's 23rd annual meeting, describing her experiences crossing over the Old Oregon Trail.

"In the springtime, coming across the Plains, all the earth is fresh and green and the way seems promising and pleasant.... The wagon train goes on and on and finally through a boundless desert with its dried up desert streams and its dry hot wind, and the merry making that characterized evening camp turns to mourning.

"As the wagons stretch out over this plain of somber hue and desert waste, the dust arises like smoke. It fills the sky and falls again on beast and wagon, tent and plain. While crossing this parched vegetation and naked earth, cattle plaintively low and call across the land, thrust their tongues from heat and thirst, and thousands die. A stench goes up that poisons the air, and the next wagon train has the cholera. Sickness comes often.

"Food sometimes fails. Tired and fretful children cry for bread. Mothers hold their little children and watch them suffer, die, and shortly leave them in a quick-made grave on the lonely desert. Mothers and wives die. Fathers and husbands die. Others lie on beds of sickness and endure through long days of dust and heat and always there is the noise of the tramping teams, the rattle of yokes and chains and wheels, and querulous noise of tired men and women and peevish children.

"You may think this picture overdrawn. But I know it truthfully depicts the horrors of some lives that were spared, and some that were sacrificed.... I can tell you this, it was not the same thrifty, well-to-do people we saw leaving their homes in the east five or six months before that finally crossed over the Cascade Mountains."

# GONE FOR GOLD

"We were living in Oregon in 1848 when gold was struck in California," wrote Anna Belknap. "All the men in the Willamette Valley went wild with gold fever.

"We had no newspapers or any reliable way to get information, so story after story made the rounds with each teller adding on a bit. The men believed everything they heard and soon most of the husbands and fathers in our neighborhood had left wives and families to travel to California and hunt the gold. I sincerely believe they thought they would be back in a couple of months with gold enough to sink a ship. We women stayed on the land claims and waited while the men chased after their dreams.

"The lure of gold was filled with danger. A man could be shot by renegades, white or Indian, at his diggings; or he might be murdered protecting his small horde of gold on the way home. Those who made it back alive and still had family and food awaiting them were the lucky ones. Gold broke up more homes in that day than alcohol ever has.

"For all of us women who stayed in Oregon while our husbands were off chasing the yellow metal, we worked hard and endured the drudgery of raising a family and building a homestead from scratch. Every morning there were the same problems to face as well as new challenges.

"If it had not been for our Indian neighbors, not many of us women could have survived in the absence of our men. We traded with the Indians for smoked salmon and fresh venison, and when we needed help they could be counted on to do whatever they were paid for, cutting cordwood or performing general farming duties. Except for one thing. No Indian would ever milk a cow. To them that was a disgraceful thing to do."

# THE LAW

Mary Gysin was one of the original leaders of the women's movement. She was a battler who challenged the political and judicial system of the Oregon Country. Born in Switzerland in 1850, Mary immigrated to Oregon and married Daniel Leonard who owned and operated a ferry on the old Oregon Trail at the John Day crossing. Their marriage was not a happy one and after a few months the Leonards became involved in a bitter divorce. Before the matter could be decided in court, Daniel was murdered and Mary was arrested and charged with shooting her husband.

Mary was jailed in The Dalles for eleven months before her attorney was able to bring her case to trial. The jury returned a verdict of not guilty and she was acquitted. But the fight to win her freedom piqued Mary's interest in the judicial system and she enrolled to study law in Seattle, Washington with Colonel J.C. Haines of the prestigious firm of Struye, Haines and McMicken. She was admitted to practice law in the Washington Territory.

Mary wanted to return to Oregon but when she applied to practice law the Oregon Supreme Court claimed it did not have authority to recognize a woman. Undaunted, Mary appealed directly to the lawmakers, and in the fall of 1885 Senate Bill 50 was passed. Again the Oregon Supreme Court tried to circumvent the intent of the law but in the end it was forced to capitulate and recognize Mary Gysin as the first woman attorney in the state of Oregon.

Mary practiced law in Portland until a few months before her death in 1912. It was not until ten years after her death that another woman was admitted to the Oregon Bar.

# PULLING TEETH

Mary Gardner fell in love with a young dentist, Dr. Skiff. Together, hand in hand, they went to Mary's father to ask his permission to wed.

"I wish to ask for your daughter's hand in marriage. We would like your blessing in this matter," Dr. Skiff told Abner Gardner.

"I cannot give my consent," Abner told him.

"But why not?" questioned Mary.

"Because he ain't a farmer," insisted her father. "He's only a dentist. How's he ever going to support you after he's pulled every tooth in the country?"

At the time, dentistry consisted simply of pulling teeth as they became decayed or abscessed. The couple, respectful of Abner's wishes, waited patiently for him to change his mind. While they marked time, wagon emigrants continued to flood into the country and Dr. Skiff was kept busy extracting teeth.

Abner made it a point to visit each new homesteading family, welcoming them and he always inquired, "What kind of shape are your teeth in?" The usual response surprised him. Nearly every adult needed the services of a dentist. Slowly Abner realized a dentist just might have a future.

"All right," he finally told his daughter and Dr. Skiff. "There's enough teeth in the country to keep you from starving. I guess the two of you can get married."

# MAIL ORDER BRIDE

For the price of a ticket and the promise of a better life in the United States, pretty Kathleen Forreststall became a mail-order bride. She departed her Irish homeland bound for Fort Klamath, Oregon and the soldier who had paid $300 for her passage.

The Atlantic crossing was rough, the ship was poorly equipped and provisions severely limited. Kathleen subsisted mainly on crackers. At the Isthmus of Panama, where the passengers were taken overland, she was able to purchase bananas.

On the voyage up the west coast Kathleen took another girl into her confidence and showed where her money was hidden, sewn into the lining of a dress. Before they reached port the money was stolen, the friendship ruined and Kathleen was stranded until the groom-to-be could be contacted and arrange to pay the stage fare.

Kathleen finally arrived at Fort Klamath and a wedding date was set for the next visit of Father Blanchett. Before the ceremony could be held the soldier was sent to Fort Walla Walla to transport supplies back to Fort Klamath. While he was gone a dance was held. Kathleen attended the dance and had a wonderful evening dancing with a number of men.

When the soldier returned and learned of Kathleen's actions he promptly called off the wedding. Several years later Kathleen married — this time for love.

# COWGIRLS

The first famous female rodeo performer was Annie Oakley. She was a sharpshooter who joined Buffalo Bill's Wild West Show in 1885 and toured North America and Europe. She introduced audiences to the idea of a cowgirl performer and soon other wild west shows featured women.

Annie Shaeffer was the first woman to officially enter a rodeo event, riding a bucking horse at the Fort Smith, Arkansas rodeo. Women were soon performing saddle bronc riding exhibitions, often riding the same horses as the men. The difference was that men rode with the stirrups free while women tied the stirrups together under the horse, supposedly to make for a safer ride.

Women were quick to become masters of trick riding and went through routines of drags, stands, vaults and occasionally passing under a horse's belly at a full gallop.

Cowgirls also competed in relay races, riding three or four horses, circling the track once with each horse. Vera McGinnes was credited with inventing the flying change, jumping from one horse to the next without ever touching the ground.

The 1920s were golden years for women participating in rodeo competitions. But at the Pendleton Round-Up of 1929 Bonnie McCarrol got hung up riding a bronc. She was tossed back and forth before finally being thrown free and landing on her neck. Bonnie died and for a long time women were not allowed to compete in rodeos because no one wanted to see another tragic accident take place in the arena.

# BRIDE AND GROOM

Cornelius Rogers came west to convert the Nez Perce Indians to Christianity. He was a member of the Lapwai Mission in Idaho until a dispute with the Reverend Henry Spalding prompted him to withdraw from missionary work.

Rogers traveled west to the Willamette Valley. Here he met Miss Satira Leslie and they were married in 1842. For their honeymoon the bride and groom decided to take a trip to the new settlement that was being built at Willamette Falls.

They enlisted four Indians to paddle a large canoe down the Willamette River. At the last minute another passenger asked if he could go along for the ride and he was granted permission to join the honeymooners.

The river was running high from recent rains but the trip was uneventful until they reached a point just above Willamette Falls. The roar of the water could clearly be heard as the four Indians steered the canoe to shore.

The man who had taken passage at the last minute tried to step onto a log that served as a landing. But he lost his balance and although he was able to grab the log and save himself his efforts tipped the canoe, partially filling it with water and sending it into the current. The Indians paddled mightily as they tried to propel the canoe toward shore, and for a moment it appeared they might succeed but then the current won the battle, sweeping the waterlogged canoe toward the falls.

Two of the Indians quit paddling, jumped in the water and saved themselves. The other two, along Mr. and Mrs. Rogers, were swept over the falls to their deaths.

# RIVER JOURNEY

Mrs. J.T. Gowdy was a pioneer of 1852. When the wagon train reached The Dalles her family chose to float the Columbia River to the Willamette Valley rather than to take the difficult trail up and over the Cascade Mountains.

Mary recalled the morning they departed, writing: "We were up early; made a breakfast of cold bread and meat with a cup of hot coffee. We couldn't cook on the flatboat, so we had to take cold food along.

"The men took the wagons apart. They put the running gear in the bottom of the boats, set the wagon boxes above and then packed all the people, like sardines, on top of all that.

"When we reached the falls at Upper Cascades people by the hundreds were crowded on a narrow strip of land at the brink of the river with a high rocky cliff at the back. We put the wagons together and piled things in and went around the portage to the Lower Cascades, a distance of five miles. When we came around the falls they had to take the wagons apart again, load them and ourselves on another flatboat. It took us to a landing at the mouth of the Sandy River.

"For the final time the wagons were put together. Everything was in, the oxen were hitched up and we pursued the last steps of our weary journey to the Willamette Valley and the home we would make there."

# THE FARMER'S WIFE

At the turn of this century the role of the western woman was undergoing a revolution of change from that of the pioneering era. Clara Waldo wrote in 1905 that the woman of that day: "...dresses better, practices physical culture, takes a little more rest, reads more magazines and books, makes herself a better companion to her children and husband, takes more outings to coast and mountains, camps with her family at the State Fair and the Chautauqua Assembly, and is in general a much more cheerful and interesting woman than she has ever been.

"With our correspondence schools, with modern languages taught by phonograph, with art reproductions for one cent apiece, with the traveling library, with current literature at club rates, with lecture courses and farmers' institutes, with stereopticon views of every famous object on the earth's surface, with Graphophone records of every fine singer, actor, speaker and orchestra; the woman on the farm is not lacking in general information.

"The rural free delivery of mail and the rural telephone are great boons to the isolated woman. She is wishing with all her heart for an enlarged parcel post, so that she may buy more freely from the city merchants.

"However, much of society's culture and polish is denied the woman on the farm. So the woman on the farm, while lacking much in 'style' and society small talk, has a comprehensive and practical knowledge of many things. She is an independent and all-around serviceable person. Indoors or out, she can 'lend a hand' where there is a need. If her husband falls ill or dies, she can manage the business of the farm and bring up the children."

# FRONTIER TEACHER

In the spring of 1851 Miss Mary Gray, along with five other single women, departed from New York by ship. Their destination was the Pacific Northwest, where they had been hired as schoolteachers.

Upon reaching the Isthmus of Panama Miss Gray wrote: "We were led down the steps on the side of our vessel to a place where a small boat approached to the nearest point. Each one was told to 'jump into that man's arms'. It did not seem possible to do so, but it was the only way. One lady waited a little too long and took a plunge into the ocean from which she was recovered."

After laying over several days in a hotel that had "an earth floor, thatched roof, no chairs and cot beds on the floor", the women were ferried over the mountains on mules. Of that experience Miss Gray wrote: "It was well for me that there were a few miles of comparatively level road at the outset, otherwise I could never have retained my seat on the mule. Being totally unused to riding, it seemed as if I should fall off at every step. Many times the trail looked so dangerous I felt very much afraid; but what could I do but go on? I could not stop my mule. The animal did not seem vicious, but only wanted to take the lead, and would do so at every opportunity."

The women took passage on the steamer *California* for the run up the Pacific side of the continent. They arrived at the mouth of the Columbia River on April 28. Miss Gray wrote: "We were taken in small boats to a point where there was a huge fallen fir tree upon which we landed and then climbing over its roots, we jumped down into the settlement of Astoria. It seemed a wild, new place, with only a small sprinkling of houses scattered among trees and huge stumps."

# UNRELENTING WOMAN

"James and I were married in Ohio. That was 1873. We had three children, a boy and two girls. I thought James was happy, that his life was fulfilled. And then he just ran out on us," recalled Mrs. Gawley.

"I went after him, traveled clear to the West, to Hoquiam, Washington. I heard he was working there. Then it was on to New Orleans. I jumped around, dragging the kids with me. At one point I must have been close to finding him because he mailed me $400. I used the money to continue my search.

"When the money was gone I went to work, sewing, washing, doing odd jobs. I raised the children alone. During that time I had offers of marriage but always refused them. I wanted to find James. I figured no task was too great for a woman if she sets her mind to it.

"I lost track of the years. But I never forgot James. There was not a day went by that I did not dream of catching him. Finally, one day out of the clear blue, a friend of his called and said James could be found in Portland, Oregon and told me his whereabouts. I went right there, confronted James on a downtown street, demanded he make past restitutions.

"Seeing him again after 25 years was quite a shock. Our youngest child was now 32. All those years passed and I never had time to grow old. I was busy trying to make a living and never giving up hope of finding James. But when I finally found him I was not so sure. The years had treated him poorly. He showed his age. After all I have gone through I decided he was probably not going to be of much use to me."

# LITTLE JOE

Little Joe was not the man he seemed to be. In fact, he was not a man at all; but that fact was not revealed until much later.

Josephine Monaghan was born in 1847 to a prominent East Coast family. As a teenager she had a love affair, became pregnant and fled to New York where her lover abandoned her. She gave birth to a son who was immediately given up for adoption. Josephine fled in disgrace. She headed west and soon discovered it was dangerous for a woman to travel alone. She began dressing like a young man and she told people her name was Joe.

Upon reaching the Idaho gold country Josephine staked a mining claim. When that failed to pay she became a sheepherder and later a cowhand. She learned to ride wild broncs and rope. Because she was so slight of stature the cowboys took to calling her Little Joe.

For seventeen years Little Joe worked and saved her money with the hope of one day buying a ranch. She entrusted her life savings to a friend who absconded with more than $3,000. But Little Joe refused to give up her dream. She took a homestead on Succor Creek in southeastern Oregon and built an outfit that included fifty horses and several hundred head of cattle. The nearest town was Rockville where Little Joe was an accepted member of the community, voting in elections and serving as a juror years before those rights were granted to women.

Little Joe died of pneumonia in 1903. As her body was prepared for burial her closely-guarded secret was revealed.

# GRANDMA WOOD

Mary Ramsey was born in Tennessee May 20, 1787. She married at 17, had four children, and moved to Georgia where her husband died in 1839.

A decade later Mary moved her family to Missouri and then brought them across the Plains in a covered wagon to Oregon. She rode the entire distance on a mare she named Martha Washington Pioneer.

At the age of 67 she married John Wood in Washington County. John had built the first frame hotel in the town of Hillsboro.

Mary outlived John and when she became a centenarian friends and relatives, who affectionately called her Grandma Wood, threw her a party. That day she reminisced about her life, telling that she had seen General George Washington and Thomas Jefferson. But she claimed the highlight of her life had been "the time Andy Jackson asked me to dance. He was the best president this country ever had. He knew how to make laws and how to enforce them. He was a fighter for what he believed in."

In 1907 Grandma Wood celebrated her 120th birthday. That fall her health finally began to fail and she planned her funeral, telling her family, "Whatever you do, don't convey my remains in no hearse. Load my coffin in a hack. I've lived as a Democrat and I'll go out in a Democratic wagon."

Grandma died the first day of 1908. Her funeral went just as she had planned, even down to the quilt she had picked to cover her coffin in the back of the hack.

# STARTING SCHOOL

Emma Sodergrin was born in Sweden in 1847. She immigrated to this country when she was nineteen and four years later she married and moved to a small log cabin on the Oregon coast.

"We were the first white family to settle in that part of the country," Emma recalled. "Gradually more and more people drifted into the area and took up land claims.

"I had three children and I wanted them to have the advantages of a school. But there were no schools and so I packed the children in a boat and traveled up the Coquille River talking settlers into signing a petition for a school.

"But the petition did not do much good because the county officials would only give money if a school was already established. I retraced my steps, went back around and asked all the folks who had signed my petition to sign a subscription paper committing to establish a school.

"The settlers came together, felled trees and a schoolhouse was constructed. I made window curtains out of flour sacks. A cedar tree was split to make benches and a table. And on the first day of school we had 13 students."

# TRAVELING EAST

Dora Bucklin remembered growing up on the plains of Nebraska and each spring watching pioneers pass her home. Their canvas-covered wagons often proclaimed, "Oregon or Bust", "Going to the Promised Land", and "Home Sweet Home".

"The people heading west were always cheerful and so very full of hope," recalled Dora. "But every fall the migration turned around and those who had become disillusioned with life in the West were returning east. These pioneers were ragged, gaunt, tired and sad.

"One time a west-bound wagon, pulled by a horse and a cow hitched together, stopped by our farm. A man, woman and baby were in the wagon. They had taken the cow along so the baby would have milk. The man tried to joke about his mismatched team. The woman just cried.

"Another instance of the outfits that traveled back over the Oregon Trail was the wagon I spotted one evening coming slowly up the road. I called to the folks and at first we could hardly believe our eyes. As they drew nearer we could see a man had hitched himself beside his horse. In the wagon were his wife and three small children.

"They spent the night with us. The man explained how one of his horses had died and related he had had two options: abandon the wagon and put his wife and children on the remaining horse, or take up the trace himself.

"Next morning Father gave the destitute family our saddle horse. The husband and his wife were so grateful they sobbed openly. After they were gone it was my turn to cry because that horse had been my pet."

# TAKEN PRISONER

The Geisel family claimed homestead land and built a little cabin on the lower Rogue River of southwestern Oregon. Their idyllic existence ended on the night of February 22, 1856.

Mary Geisel, who was 13 years old at the time, recalled what happened that night. "There came a knock on the door. Father opened it. There were Indians and they wanted to come in. There was a struggle. The Indians were trying to kill Father with their knives. Mother heard them and ran to help. One grabbed and held her while the others finished killing Father.

"The Indians took Mother, my three-week-old sister Anna, and myself outdoors and then went back and killed my three brothers: John, nine; Henry, seven; and Andrew, five. They set fire to the house and we watched it burn until we were taken away.

"We didn't know what the Indians were going to do to us, nor how soon they would become angry and kill us. After two weeks the settlers arranged a trade and Mother and my sister were traded for blankets but there were not enough blankets so the conference broke up and Mother and my baby sister went with the settlers and I had to return to the Indian camp.

"That night I tried to sleep, but my dreams were filled with dread because I was all alone in a camp of hostiles who were planning on killing all the settlers on the coast. The next day a trade for my release was arranged and you can only imagine my joy that I was finally free."

# A CHILD'S MEMORIES

The Sager family started west over the Oregon Trail but along the way Henry Sager and his wife Naomi died of mountain fever. They left behind seven orphaned children.

"We seven children were cared for by the other emigrants," related Matilda Jane Sager. "When we reached the Whitman Mission, Dr. and Mrs. Whitman took us in.

"But then came the events of November 29, 1847 and our foster parents, Dr. and Mrs. Whitman, and two of my brothers, were massacred by Indians as were others at the mission. The Indians captured us and we were released only after a ransom was paid.

"I was shuffled from one Willamette Valley family to another, and so were my brothers and sisters. We lost touch with each other. I remember one time the man of the house where I was staying rode up to the cabin and called to me to get my sunbonnet and get up behind him.

"Children didn't ask questions in those days. They obeyed. We rode to Hillsboro to where a crowd was assembled. Presently a man was brought out and hanged. I was horrified.

"On the way back home my foster father told me, 'I brought you to see the hanging to impress on your mind what happens to people who do not mind their elders and do exactly what they are told.'"

# WHEELBARROW WOMAN

A woman calling herself Roxy Dunbar appeared in Baker Valley one day in 1931. She hired a local teamster to haul her and two large bundles to the breaks of the Snake River. From there she started down into the deepest canyon on the North American continent, carrying one bundle a short distance, setting it down and returning for the other.

At one of the scattered homesteads a woman took pity on Roxy and gave her a wheelbarrow. Roxy loaded her worldly possessions into this wheelbarrow and pushed it downhill to the Snake River. Upon reaching the cabin occupied by old man Van Cleve she found him dreadfully sick and he requested that she stay in his cabin and try to nurse him back to health. But in spite of her efforts Van Cleve died.

Roxy decided to stay at the Van Cleve place. She worked to make the house more livable, set new posts in the corral and planted a big garden. She used a pick and shovel to tunnel into the hillside and build a root cellar that she filled with produce from the garden.

Roxy lived at the old Van Cleve place all during the depression years. Then one day she loaded her belongings in the wheelbarrow and started up and out of the canyon. At Baker City she discarded the wheelbarrow and bought a ticket on the train. Without explaining why she had gone to the end of civilization or why she had returned, Roxy Dunbar departed and was never heard from again.

# MY DOLL

When several tribes east of the Cascade Mountains went on the warpath in 1855 pioneer Sam Warfield made the decision to leave his family and go fight the Indians.

Sam was assigned to Company H and his commander, Lieutenant Colonel James Kelly, ordered his men to march on a village of Walla Walla Indians. Chief Peu-peu-mox-mox and six warriors rode out to meet Kelly's troops.

During the council Kelly related how the Indians had stolen cattle and burned homes of the settlers. The chief said these things were done by some of the young warriors against his orders. He offered restitution but Kelly said that in addition to payment, the Indians had to surrender their arms and ammunition, furnish beef for the soldiers and give up a certain number of horses.

Peu-peu-mox-mox agreed to the terms. But when he started to leave Kelly feared the chief would not keep his word and demanded the chief be held hostage until the conditions had been met.

Sam's daughter, Emma Warfield, related what happened next. "According to what I was told, Peu-peu-mox-mox tried to seize my father's rifle. Father killed him, and then he took the scalp of the Indian chief.

"When Father returned from the war he gave me the scalp of Peu-peu-mox-mox. Mother sewed the scalp on the head of a rag doll. For years and years that was my favorite doll."

# BROTHER

Henry Chapman was a frail and sickly child. His sister Vittwia watched over him and even slept on the floor beside his bed so she could tend his needs during the night. But when Henry was 20 years old he announced he was joining a wagon train bound for Oregon.

"The others laughed at me when, upon hearing the news, I cried out, 'Poor Henry! Who will cover your feet and give you your medicine if I do not go along?' Vittwia recalled.

"Henry went off to Oregon without me. It was while he was in the Rogue River country that he shot a grizzly bear and carelessly did not reload his rifle. He went to examine the dead bear, which was a huge one, but as he approached the bear came alive and attacked my poor brother, mauling him terribly.

"Two men who had been hunting with Henry heard his screams. They doubled back and killed the grizzly. They thought Henry was dead and tied him across his horse to bring him in for a Christian burial. But the motion of the horse caused Henry to start breathing again and by the grace of God the doctor in Jacksonville was able to save my brother's life, although he was horribly disfigured.

"After this tragedy I felt it was my responsibility to come out west. My first duty was to Henry. Over all the years I cared for Henry I did not marry or have a sweetheart because I never wanted my brother to feel as though he were playing second fiddle."

31

# HARD TIMES

"My parents discussed loading up the wagon and going all the way to Oregon, but they never did," recalled Jessie Gentry. "They settled in western Nebraska and built a dugout near a small creek. We had a fireplace and a little stove for cooking. For fuel us kids gathered dry chips from the cow pasture to burn, and when corn slipped to eight cents a bushel we burned corncobs.

"Our furniture consisted of a table and two kegs to sit on, one for Father and the other for Mother. Us kids stood at the table and didn't think anything about it because we were used to it. Our parents said we were lucky to have what we had. They said when they were first married they sat on pumpkins with the food spread out on a canvas tarp on the bed.

"We were 75 miles from the closest town. I remember one time Mother had a toothache and there was no relief for it until spring. She had to wait until her baby was born and a month old before we made the long trip to the dentist.

"I know we had it better than a lot of folks who lived out where we did. There was one neighboring family who had a real tough go of things. The man of the house was terribly sick with tuberculosis. He could not do a lick of work around the place. All he could do was to cuddle close by the fire and twist together bunches of hay that he fed into the stove. And the children had no shoes except cloth moccasins their mother sewed for them.

"In comparison to this family we lived a relatively comfortable existence."

# LADY AND THE POET

Minnie Myrtle Dyer was a rising poet who drew her inspiration from the rugged coastline of the Pacific Northwest. In 1862 Cincinnatus Miller, who was to gain renown as Joaquin Miller, came to visit the young woman and within a week they were married. Eight years and three children later, Miller decided his own poetry was more important than his family. He departed and a divorce soon followed. He went on to become idolized in Europe as the "Poet of the Sierra". And while his personal popularity soared, his family, living on Elk River near Port Orford, suffered. In order to survive Minnie had to farm out her children to family and friends.

Minnie took to the lecture circuit, her favorite topic being "Joaquin Miller, the Poet and the Man". She told intimate details of the private life they had shared and the crux of her speech was that Joaquin might be a great poet, but as a human being he had serious shortcomings.

For a time her lectures were well-attended but the public soon became bored with the trivial rehashing of her shattered marriage. Destitute, ill and alone, Minnie traveled to New York City where Joaquin was living at the time. He came to her aid, providing assistance and shelter. He summoned a physician but it was too late. Minnie died and was buried in Evergreen Cemetery, a continent away from the Pacific Ocean, her first love and the inspiration for her early poetry.

# BAD LUCK

Jim and Lucy had a run of bad luck. They came west, took a homestead and tried to hang on through several years of drought. Jim, to augment their meager income, worked for a neighbor. And then Lucy developed inflammatory rheumatism and it progressed to the point she was confined to bed.

All that winter Lucy was unable to tend the fire, but with plenty of bedding she stayed comfortably warm while Jim was working. When Jim came home he built up the fire, tended the household chores and cooked.

One of the things they craved, and had not eaten since Lucy became ill, was light bread. Several mornings Jim had mixed dough, planning to bake it when he came home. But the dough did not rise because the homestead cabin was too cold.

Lucy had an inspiration. One morning, before he left for work, she had Jim tuck the bowl of bread dough in bed beside her. Her body warmth allowed the yeast to work. That evening they enjoyed a tasty treat of light bread.

This small accomplishment meant the world to Lucy. She felt she was once again contributing to the household. The following spring she utilized her confinement by having Jim tuck two dozen eggs in bed with her. She tended the eggs like a conscientious hen; keeping them warm, turning them a quarter turn each day, making sure she never crushed one of the delicate shells.

Twenty-three eggs hatched. By that point Lucy was well enough to get out of bed and tend the fluffy yellow chicks.

# BEFORE WELFARE

"Things were different in the old days," related Kelsey Congor, whose family was among the early day settlers in the Pacific Northwest.

"You see, those who came here first and cleared land made good money by selling produce to those who came later. They got good prices for what they shipped out, too. The pioneers were very kind and liberal to newcomers, sharing beef, pork, fruit, and whatall, until the newcomers could stand on their own two feet.

"Here is something for people to think about. Back in the early days there were no relief agencies and neighbors had to look out for each other. It was a very rare instance when the local government was called on to come to the aid of a particular resident in dire circumstances.

"I recall one incident where county commissioners gave a widow a lump sum payment of one hundred dollars. She went out and bought herself the most expensive dress she could find and even splurged to the tune of five dollars for a new hat. Five dollars was an unheard of amount of money for a single piece of clothing.

"Some of the ladies in the local area criticized the widow woman for her extravagance. But to my way of thinking that was the best investment the county ever made for, you see, the widow woman paraded around in that splendid hat and she caught the attention of a certain well-to-do gentleman. They married and went to live in Clark County, Washington. That's just the way things worked in the old days."

# MOTHER JOSEPH

Esther Pariseau was born on a farm near Montreal in 1823. From her father, Joseph, she learned farming and carpentry skills and at the age of twenty, when she joined the Sisters of Charity of Providence in Montreal, she took her father's name.

Mother Joseph dedicated her life to the poor, hungry, homeless and unfortunate. She was assigned to the West and traveled overland by rail, boat and on foot. She arrived at Fort Vancouver in December 1856.

She immediately began to put all her skills to good use. She helped the pioneers construct buildings, cared for the sick, taught school, did laundry, gardened and sewed. She was a woman of seemingly boundless energy, enthusiasm and talent.

When there was not enough money to perform the works of charity and mercy, Mother Joseph went on tours of settlements, military outposts and mining camps from British Columbia to Colorado. She endured blizzards, attacks by wild animals and threats by bandits, returning home with the money necessary to complete good work and to undertake new projects.

In her time Mother Joseph was credited as architect, financier, and construction boss. She was instrumental in the building of eleven hospitals, seven academies, five Indian schools, and two orphanages.

Mother Joseph died in 1902 of a brain tumor. Half a century later she was recognized and honored by the Institute of American Architecture as the Pacific Northwest's first architect.

# NIGHTCAP

"We were living along the Columbia River," related Mrs. Bucky, an early day pioneer. "It so happened that two officers from an English vessel had been on a hunting expedition when night overtook them. They stopped by our cabin and asked for a night's lodging. We were not prepared for company but we told them we would make them as comfortable as possible with a bed on the floor.

"I fixed them something to eat and then we sat around a big, bright fire talking until quite late. Both gentlemen were very cultured and splendid conversationalists. Finally we all retired for the night, they to their pallet on the floor and my husband and I to our small bedroom. The wall between the rooms was very thin, covered with boards that had cracks between. One could easily hear from one room to the other, hear every word.

"I happened to overhear one of the gentlemen comment he wished he had a nightcap. I thought about getting them a nightcap of mine, but my caps were so plain and these were such aristocratic-looking gentlemen that I did not wish to insult them.

"Some time passed and I heard one of them ask, 'Are you awake?' and the other answered that he indeed was still awake. The first spoke again, 'I do not believe I can go to sleep without a nightcap.'

"That propelled me into action. I got out of bed, took two of my nightcaps, made of white muslin with strings to tie under the chin, and going to the door I put my hand through and said, 'Gentlemen, here are two nightcaps. They are plain and rather small, but perhaps you can use them.'

"All was quiet for a moment and then I heard the faint sound of suppressed laughter. And an instant later the cabin resounded with hearty laughter. Eventually one of the gentlemen informed me they were desirous of a different type of nightcap — of the liquid spirit variety."

# THE FLOOD

The spring of 1861 brought a Chinook wind that melted the snow pack in the high Cascade Mountains and sent the Willamette River over its banks.

The George family lived beside the river. When the rising water reached the foundation they moved to the second floor. All through the night the house creaked and groaned. With the arrival of morning's light Mr. George, fearing the house would soon be swept off its foundation, made his decision. He brought a rowboat alongside the house and directed his wife and children to climb aboard.

Away from the house the overloaded rowboat was at the mercy of the surging current. A whirlpool suddenly opened like a huge gaping mouth, sucking the rowboat down and dumping the George family into the brown swirling water. Mrs. George tried to grab her children but they were wrenched from her grasp. She called out repeatedly, "Help! Help! Help!"

Her husband caught his wife and since she could not swim he removed his belt, looped it over an exposed tree branch and fastened it around her wrists to prevent her from being swept away. He promised to return and swam away in a vain effort to find the children.

Neighbors eventually rescued Mrs. George. By then she was hysterical. And little wonder because while she hung there with her arms tied around the limb, her two daughters had been swept near her and she had been forced to listen to their pleas for help. Her entire family was swept away and drowned in the terrible flood of 1861.

# ONE-ROOM SCHOOL

Gladys Beckley was reared in the Willamette Valley. The first time she ventured east of the mountains was after accepting a teaching position in Virginia Valley, a remote school in Harney County.

"When I first arrived, as I saw what a lonely place it was, I cried. But I was being paid $125 a month, which was more than my college professors were making," recalled Gladys. "I was determined to stick out the contract year.

"I soon discovered that my duties were not limited to teaching reading, writing and arithmetic to the twenty ranch children, who ranged in ages from six to fourteen. I was also responsible for janitorial duties as well as helping the first and second graders saddle and bridle their horses every afternoon. I was a city girl. I had never saddled or bridled a horse in my life. But I had no choice but to learn how to do such things.

"Every morning I rose early and started a fire so the building would be warm when the children arrived. Next I would pump a bucket of water. Each child had a cup hung from a nail pounded in the wall. They were supposed to use a common dipper to fill their cups but once in a while I would catch one of the boys drinking from the dipper and for punishment I made him freshen the outhouse."

The one-room schoolhouse was the center of social life in Virginia Valley. Dances and potluck suppers were held there. Ranchers sent mail to school with their children. The letters were placed on the window ledge in the hall and during the day, anyone riding past the school going to Princeton or Crane stopped to pick up the mail.

Gladys discovered she enjoyed the wide-open spaces of the High Desert and the slow pace of life in Virginia Valley. She married a local rancher and had a successful career teaching several generations of ranchers' sons and daughters.

# THE LIFE OF A PIONEER

At the turn of the century a letter was found that described early-day life in the West. The writer was a woman, but her identity has never been discovered.

She wrote: "I made a long, tedious trip across the Plains in '53, but by no means was it uninteresting to a young girl. We reached the Willamette Valley and I was told that if I chose to marry I would get 180 acres of land. So, of course, I married. But my husband went to the Salmon River mines of Idaho and I was left alone. After my husband returned we concluded to take a homestead.

"At first he 'bached in a little log cabin that he built on the place. When he came to visit me in our old home I said to him, 'I am going with you.' He told me the cabin was too small, but I told him, 'Where you live, I live. I am going.'

"On the 3rd day of July we reached the little cabin that did not even have chinking between the logs. We put our things inside and then my husband returned to bring up the cattle and I was left alone in the woods. Darkness came on. I sat down to read a chapter in the Bible but all at once the wild cats began to screech, the owls to whoo-whoo and the wolves to howl. I jumped into bed almost frightened to death.

"When my husband returned I proposed to him that I sell my gold watch for lumber to build a real house. He seriously objected but I said I would never wear a gold watch and not have a decent house to live in. Soon after, a man came along who had a portable sawmill and I asked him if he would give me lumber to build a house in exchange for my watch. He said he would. We built the house, made a real home there in the wilderness and we were happy."

# DESPERATE

"I was one of ten children. Father died on the way across the Plains. We landed in the Willamette Valley with no money so Mother would go down to where the ships came in and take in washing. Then she started a boarding house. When a man, a cook in a restaurant, offered to marry me — I was 14 and he was 44 — Mother thought I had better take him. So I did," Elvina Apperson recalled.

"At that point in time we had slavery of Negroes in the South, and slavery of wives all over the country. Saloons were wherever there were enough people to make it pay. What could a girl do to protect herself, especially if her husband drank like mine did? I still shudder when I think of my girlhood, having to live with that man. When he was drinking, and he was always drinking, he would often beat me until I thought I could not stand it.

"One time he came to my mother's house, where I had taken refuge. I locked the door. He tried to climb in the window, but I held him out. This enraged him so he took out his pistol and shot at me. The bullet passed just over my head but the glass fell on me and scared me so I dropped to the floor. He looked in and saw me lying on the floor; thinking he had killed me, he put the end of the pistol barrel into his mouth and pulled the trigger. I was a widow."

According to Elvina her life story had a happy ending. "When I was 20 I married a fine man, a steamboat engineer. This time I married for love and my husband loved me. He always treated me good."

# THE FLAG

General Lee had led the rebels to victory at Fredericksburg and was advancing toward Gettysburg. A continent away, in Oregon's Grande Ronde Valley, a group of southern sympathizers passed a law forbidding the flying of the Stars and Stripes.

Mrs. Harriet Lewis, a resident of the Grande Ronde Valley, called several of her friends together to discuss the law. She told them, "If we remain silent we condone the rebels. We must fly Old Glory."

"But we do not have a flag," commented one of the women.

"Then we shall sew a flag," vowed Mrs. Lewis. "I have three yards of bright red material I was saving to make a shirt for my husband. We can use a sheet for the stars. Who has something blue?"

Miss Martha Koger spoke. "I have a blue riding skirt. It is the finest garment I own, and my favorite, but I think this idea of Harriet's is important."

The women used the riding skirt for a field of blue for the stars and added the red and white stripes. On the 4th of July, 1863, they proudly flew the flag from a pole on Hendershott's Point. There was not a rebel who was man enough to step forward and cut it down in the face of the determined women.

On that date General Lee's army, after sustaining losses of 20,000 men, retreated under the cover of darkness. This marked the turning point in the Civil War.

# THE LADY

In 1849 Mrs. Polly Leabo and her family came west over the Oregon Trail. When they reached the Blue Mountains the men went hunting and the women remained in camp. Mrs. Leabo and the other women in the wagon train were preparing dinner over campfires when one of the children hollered, "Someone's coming!"

Mrs. Leabo glanced up. She was expecting to see her husband or one of the other men with a deer slung over a packhorse. Instead she saw a lone Indian. And this Indian was not wearing a stitch of clothing. He marched in a straight line for Mrs. Leabo's fire and stood there hungrily eyeing the browning meat.

Mrs. Leabo was a very prim and proper lady. The other women stood watching, fearful she might do something drastic. But she paid the naked Indian absolutely no mind and kept turning the meat with her large butcher knife.

When the steaks were cooked and ready to be placed on the platter Mrs. Leabo removed them with the butcher knife, one by one. When only a single steak remained, the Indian reached out to grab it. Mrs. Leabo, using the blunt side of the knife, cracked the Indian across the knuckles. He let out a surprised howl, dropped the meat and ran from camp.

When the men returned and heard what had transpired in their absence, Mr. Leabo questioned his wife, "Polly, whatever possessed you to do that? Why didn't you let him have the meat? If you have angered his tribe they will massacre us."

"I do not care," bristled Mrs. Leabo. "I would rather have died than further endure the sight of a naked man standing at my fire."

# SAVING THE CHICKENS

One spring morning in 1908 Mrs. Caldwell, who lived with her husband on the Wingfield Ranch near Adel, Oregon, was washing dishes at the kitchen sink. The window was open and a slight breeze was blowing warm air into the room.

All at once she heard sounds of a terrible commotion in the barnyard, loud and excited squawking and the wild beating of wings. Mrs. Caldwell immediately suspected that some wild animal was after one of her plump hens. Without considering any danger to herself she flung open the screen door and flew outside, shouting and waving a dish towel.

The offending animal was a coyote. It turned on her and Mrs. Caldwell, trying to reverse her forward momentum, lost her balance and fell. In an instant the coyote was snarling and snapping at her face. She tried to push the animal away. Instinctively she grabbed his exposed throat and squeezed. She felt the windpipe collapse. The coyote gave a shudder and then lay still.

It was several minutes before Mrs. Caldwell collected her strength and was able to roll from beneath the lifeless form of the coyote. She stumbled to the house, dressed her wounds and said a prayer of thanks.

That afternoon after Mr. Caldwell had listened to the story of his wife's recklessness, he shook his head and reprimanded her for not having used the loaded rifle he always kept beside the door. He skinned the carcass of the coyote, tanned the hide and gave it to his wife as a souvenir of what she ever after referred to as, "the most blood-curdling experience of my life."

# TERRIBLE TRAIL

Lucy Hall was a young girl when she started west with her parents. In later years she wrote of the crossing: "We departed Independence, Missouri, the 15th day of May, 1845. The first part of the journey was uneventful. But west from Fort Laramie we had several encounters with Indians. We were attacked three times but no harm was done.

"At Fort Boise we were met by Stephen Meek. He talked a number of people, my folks included, into following him over a cutoff from the normal route of the Oregon Trail. This route crossed the desert and most of those who agreed to follow his lead did so because they owned large droves of cattle and were a little afraid of the hostile Indian country that Meek said we would have to pass through if we stayed true to the trail. It was decided that we would trust our fate to Meek.

"From that day on we had a hard time of it; we suffered from lack of water, the stock gave out, provisions were scarce, and many in the company were sick and dying with mountain fever. I saw many persons buried without the benefit of coffins. We were lost in the desert. We wandered aimlessly. The day before we reached the Deschutes River we were forsaken by our guide. We ferried across the river in a wagon box, swimming all the teams and loose stock.

"Our hearts were made to rejoice when our men, who were scouting the way, brought the glad news that they had spied the Columbia River. It was a cause for great rejoicing.

"We reached the small settlement of The Dalles and were given provisions; each family received dried peas, potatoes and a peck of wheat. Oh, what a feast we had!"

# SARAH WINNEMUCCA

Sarah Winnemucca, a Paiute Indian, was sent away to a Catholic mission school in California to be instructed in the ways of civilization. When she returned to Nevada she tried to convince her tribe they could co-exist with the white man. But in 1872 the government moved the Paiutes from their native home at Pyramid Lake, Nevada to the Malheur Reservation in Oregon. To draw attention to the hardship this move caused her people, Sarah traveled to Washington, D.C. While she was away the Paiutes, led by her father Chief Winnemucca, became involved in the Bannock War. Sarah came home and convinced her father and other members of her tribe to abandon the warpath and return to the Malheur Reservation.

The government made promises to the Indians who returned but soon reneged on those promises. After the war the Paiutes were force-marched overland to the Yakima Reservation in the Washington Territory and held as prisoners. The Paiutes blamed Sarah for their troubles, but by remaining with them through the difficult times and demanding food, clothing and blankets from the government she was able to regain their confidence.

Sarah wrote a book, *Life Amoung the Paiutes: Their Wrongs and Claims*. This book strongly criticized the Indian Bureau and Sarah was asked to return to Washington, D.C., and help draft a bill that would allow the Paiute tribe a reservation.

This legislation was passed but never implemented. The tribe blamed Sarah for selling out to the white man and she lived the rest of her days as an outcast, consumed by despair that she could not help her people. She died of tuberculosis at the age of 48.

# WHERE MAMMA IS

"In September 1851 I was riding to Forest Grove where I was then engaged in teaching," wrote Miss E.M. Wilson. "Throughout the Willamette Valley there were only trails and very few roads of any kind.

"The settlers who were few and far between had corrals for cattle and horses and fields of grain; but nowhere could a fence be found on either side of the way. The day waned; I met no one; I passed no one. It was a delightful ride, though lonely. Several times from adjoining thickets I saw the faces of deer steadily gazing at me with their penetrating eyes.

"I was still many miles from my destination and very tired. I decided that if I should come upon a cabin I would stop and see if it would be possible to obtain supper. As I turned the bend of a large hill I came in sight of a man plowing in the open at some distance. There was a cabin, and a fence enclosing a piece of land for gardening.

"Two children, about 4 and 6 years of age, were standing by a rude stile. I asked them to tell their mother that I wanted to speak with her. They made no reply, but continued to stare at me. 'Go call Mamma,' said I. There was no response. I then dismounted, wondering that no motive of interest or curiosity had caused the cabin door to open, but still all was silent. I said to the oldest child, 'Take me where Mamma is.' She readily took my hand and led me through the tall rye grass and stopped by a newly-made grave there by the little cabin."

# MOTHER LODE

The spring of 1847 Robert and Jane Caufield started west over the Oregon Trail with two heavily loaded wagons. They planned to open a store when they reached Oregon.

During the crossing they encountered unfriendly Indians, flooding rivers, and lack of feed for the oxen. By the time they started the last leg over the Cascades on the Barlow Trail, the oxen were in terrible shape. Several died and the wagons could go no farther.

Robert walked to the Willamette Valley. He was gone a week and during that time Jane stayed with the wagons. It snowed and every night the wolves howled. Robert returned with several ox teams and they were able to finally reach Oregon City, six months after leaving St. Joe.

The Caufields opened a store and were adjusting to their new life when word came that gold had been found at Sutter's Mill in California. Robert caught the gold fever and took passage on the first ship sailing south.

Jane was left in charge of the store. She bought wheat from the farmers, had it ground and sent the flour to the miners in California where she realized great profits. When Robert returned he had very little to show for his wandering; but he found that his wife Jane had been tremendously successful as a businesswoman. She had been the one who struck the mother lode.

# OREGON COWGIRL

Ella Lazinka was an Eastern Oregon cowgirl. She won the World Championship in the cowgirl relay race at the Pendleton Round-Up in 1912. The following year she returned to defend her crown.

The cowgirls' relay race was run over a three-day period. The contestants raced two miles each day, changing horses every half-mile. They were required to mount, dismount, unsaddle and saddle, without assistance.

Ella won the first day. Bertha Blanchett, a cowgirl from Los Angeles, took an early lead the second day and Ella was never able to close the gap. They entered the third day in a dead heat, tied at ten minutes and ten seconds.

At the start of the third leg of the race Ella jumped ahead and stayed in the lead until her horse started bucking. It cost her valuable time to bring him under control, jump to the ground, loosen the cinch, slip off the saddle and make the exchange. She gave chase to Bertha, who by then was flying down the straightaway.

Coming into the third exchange Ella had nearly drawn even with Bertha. The crowd was cheering wildly for the local girl. But bad luck struck again. Ella's horse continued to run past the exchange point. It ran to a gate and stopped in a four-footed slide. Ella kept going, over the horse's head and over the gate. She got up, dusted herself off and continued with the race.

Bertha was the easy winner. She crossed the finish line to a smattering of applause. The loudest cheer of the day erupted 59 seconds later when the local girl, Miss Ella Lazinka, barreled past the main grandstand.

# HOSPITALITY

Elizabeth Kelly was baking bread and the sweet aroma wafted around the little log cabin and drifted out the doorway. The door was nothing more than a buffalo hide hung over the opening.

Elizabeth's husband John was several miles away, cutting and splitting rails. Elizabeth thought she was alone and she busied herself with baking and chores. She thought she heard voices and, lifting a corner of the buffalo hide and peeking outside, she was shocked to see a group of Indians sitting on the ground in front of the doorway. Their faces were painted.

Elizabeth dropped the corner of the buffalo hide and returned to her inside work. Sunlight suddenly flooded the room and when she turned she immediately recognized the figure of John outlined in the doorway. He spoke with an urgent tone, "Food! Quickly!"

John scooped up loaves of the cooling bread, grabbed a pitcher of milk, and ducked through the doorway. He broke the bread and distributed it among the Indians. They dipped chunks of bread in the milk and ate with relish. When their hunger was satisfied they departed.

As soon as they were gone Elizabeth asked, "Why in the world did you give away all our food?"

"Didn't you see the way they were painted? Those braves are on the war path," John replied.

That day Elizabeth and John watched smoke rising here and there as their neighbors' homes were burned to the ground before the rampaging Indians.

# COUGAR RUG

"In the middle of the night one of our pigs let out a terrified squeal. I jumped out of bed, grabbed up a candle and went charging outside. My husband was right behind me, rifle in hand," recalled Sophia McKinney.

"When I reached the barnyard the candlelight revealed a big cougar. It was humped up, protecting its kill, one of our pigs. I was shocked but snapped right out of it when my husband shouted at me to hold the light nearer to the cougar. I moved forward a foot or two.

"Again my husband urged me to get closer, saying he was afraid to shoot and only wound the beast. I took a step and I suppose the cougar became provoked because it jumped on me, knocking me down and rolling me over and over. My light went out. The cougar ran away.

My husband was disgusted with the way things turned out and a little perturbed at me for not holding the candle so he could sight his rifle. But we got another chance the following evening when the intruder returned for another pig. This time when my husband went after it, the cougar climbed out on a limb over the creek. It was too dark to see much but my husband followed the animal and managed to get off a shot.

"The cougar fell off the limb into the water, but somehow swam ashore and crawled into a cave. By then my husband was so peeved that he crawled in after it. The cougar tried to come out but my husband shoved the barrel of the rifle against its throat and pulled the trigger, killing the cougar. From the tip of its nose to the tip of its tail the cougar measured ten feet. We tanned the hide and made it into a rug."

# THOSE WERE THE DAYS

"We started west in the spring of 1864 with three yoke of oxen and one yoke of cows hitched to a wagon. I was but a girl of 15 years old at the time, " related Phoebe Hulser.

"The cows were a godsend, furnishing us milk until we struck the alkali country, where the pulling was hard and the feed poor. After that we had to go without milk on our corn meal mush.

"There were upwards of 100 wagons in our wagon train. But the faster wagons pulled away and we were left with those traveling slower. By the time we reached Idaho the stock was going downhill fast. Father made the decision we would lay over for the winter. We took up residence in Idaho Falls and operated a boarding house for miners. It was my job to serve food and to help with kitchen duties. That winter I was invited to attend a number of dances but Father didn't hold with dancing and so I was not allowed to go.

"Come spring we yoked up our cattle and once more headed westward. When we reached Camas Valley, Oregon we had to leave the wagon and pack over the mountains to a place on the Coquille River. We wintered there, came out in the spring, and by then Father had decided he liked Missouri better than Oregon. He announced the family was returning to Missouri. But by that time I had met James Newton and instead of going with the family I stayed and James and I married.

"It has been better than sixty years since I crossed the Plains, but I can shut my eyes and still see the sights we saw and hear the songs we sang around the campfire. My, my, those certainly were the good old days."

# LIVERPOOL LIZ

Her given name was Elizabeth Smith but most everyone called her Liverpool Liz. She was blue-eyed, pretty and dressed conservatively except for an expensive diamond necklace that she affectionately referred to as "my little bauble".

Liz was the proprietor of the Senate Saloon on First Street in Portland, Oregon. The Senate Saloon was a favorite haunt for sailors from the seven seas. In addition to the bar there was a large dance floor and a second story arranged in cribs for the working girls. Occasionally a customer unfamiliar with the arrangement called for a round of drinks for the house. Liz pressed a button which rang a buzzer upstairs and dance hall girls and sailors came charging down the stairs clamoring to be included in the free round of drinks. Champagne was stocked for just such occasions and the man who was the butt of the joke could easily drop a month's wages on a single round of drinks.

Liz employed Tattoo Kelley as the bouncer. He was a big man with red and blue eagles, snakes, ships, hearts and flowers tattooed on his muscular arms and across his burly chest. He ruled the bar with an iron fist.

Soon after the turn of the 20th Century the days of the sailing ships and the large crews needed to man them came to an end. Steamships came to rule the seas. As a result Liz was forced to lock the swinging doors of the Senate Saloon. She died penniless and is buried in a pauper's grave at Lone Fir cemetery.

# MOTHERS' HELPERS

Mrs. E.B. Caine of Indianola, Nebraska, was nearly 80 years old when she took time to recall ways pioneer women of her mother's day used to save time.

She remembered, "One woman told Mother she would make the most of hectic days by putting the big baby in one end of the cradle and the little baby in the other. As the big baby played, it kept jiggling the cradle and kept the little baby content.

"There was another neighbor who used to claim she would put her baby in a high chair, smear molasses on its fingers and give it a feather to play with. According to her, this would keep a baby busy and the mother had hours of uninterrupted time to get all her household chores done.

"But probably the most unique method to save time on a busy day was the woman who confided to Mother that she would place her baby in the cradle and give it a sizable chunk of fat meat to suck on. She tied a string to the meat and attached the other end of the string to the baby's toe. That way if the baby happened to swallow and choke on the meat, it would start in kicking and that action would pull the meat out."

# THE VOTE

Abigail Scott Duniway, an Oregon Trail pioneer of 1852, is considered the person most responsible for bringing the right to vote to the western woman. She claimed, "As I had been blessed with a harmonious marriage, and enjoyed the natural ability to express my ideas on paper in a somewhat marked degree, it devolved upon me to voice the opinions of many women who were too timid or were not allowed by their husbands to speak for themselves."

Abigail was born in 1834 on an Illinois farm. One of her earliest memories was of her mother saying upon the birth of her ninth child, "Poor baby girl. Some day she will be a woman and a woman's lot is so hard."

Abigail married, had four children and wrote a small novel, *Captain Gray's Companion*. She helped establish the Oregon State Equal Suffrage Association, founded a newspaper dedicated to equal rights, and began a lecture tour of the western states. She traveled by rail, riverboat, stagecoach and horseback.

At her lectures Abigail would tell the audience, mostly women, that, "All the laws recognize the husband and wife as 'one', and the husband is that 'one'. The wife is legally 'dead' ... now is the time for women to rise up and secure their full and complete enfranchisement."

In 1869 the women of Wyoming were the first to be given equal political rights. It was not until the 1890s that Colorado, Utah and Idaho followed suit. The men of Oregon finally succumbed to Abigail's fiery determination and in 1912 Oregon women were granted the right to vote.

Rick Steber's Tales of the Wild West Series is available in hardbound and paperback books featuring illustrations by Don Gray, as well as audio narrated by Dallas McKennon. Current titles in the series include:

OREGON TRAIL  Vol. 1 *
PACIFIC COAST  Vol. 2 *
INDIANS  Vol. 3 *
COWBOYS  Vol. 4 *
WOMEN OF THE WEST  Vol. 5 *
CHILDREN'S STORIES  Vol. 6 *
LOGGERS  Vol. 7 *
MOUNTAIN MEN  Vol. 8 *
MINERS  Vol. 9 *
GRANDPA'S STORIES  Vol. 10
PIONEERS  Vol. 11
CAMPFIRE STORIES  Vol. 12
TALL TALES  Vol. 13
GUNFIGHTERS  Vol. 14
GRANDMA'S STORIES  Vol. 15
*Available on Audio Tape

**Other books written by Rick Steber —**

| | |
|---|---|
| NO END IN SIGHT | HEARTWOOD |
| BUY THE CHIEF A CADILLAC | ROUNDUP |
| BUCKAROO HEART | LAST OF THE PIONEERS |
| NEW YORK TO NOME | TRACES |
| WILD HORSE RIDER | RENDEZVOUS |

If unavailable at local retailers, write directly to the publisher for a free catalog.

**Bonanza Publishing**
Box 204
Prineville, Oregon 97754